SURVIVING a NARCISSIST

How I Overcame Mental Torture and Heartache

Valencia Michelle Dore

All scriptures quoted are taken from the King James Version, American Standard Version, English Standard Version and the New International Version of the Bible App.

Cover by Jamar Hargrove
Photo by Woody Martin and Lemuel Ryan
Edited by Sarah Fox of The Bookish Fox

Self-Published via Kindle Direct Publishing
Printed in the United States of America.

Personal website: www.loveyouselffoundation.com
Facebook page: www.facebook.com/loveyourselffoundation/ and
www.facebook.com/overcomersgoalachiever/

ISBN: 978-1-72301-876-3

DEDICATION

My lovely children

To Maliq, Alexia, and Jeval. My three miracles whom I always push hard for. If it weren't for them, I think I would have given up on life a long time ago.

My parents

To my mother, Laurena Millard, and father, Michael Dore, for being my biggest advocates. My parents always encouraged me to be the best I could always be.

CONTENTS

1
INTRODUCTION

This book reflects the life I lived with a narcissist. The names of everyone involved were changed to protect myself. This book is not meant to bash anyone. I am simply sharing a piece of my story. I say "a piece" because if I were to write everything, I will need two books. The main purpose is to encourage someone else who may be going through the same thing I went through, to not make the same mistake and stay stuck in a relationship they can clearly see is dead. There are too many females out there staying in relationships that they know they should let go of. Then when they had enough then someone ends up dead and that's something you can't come back from.

God has intended for us to live a healthy and prosperous life, not one filled with hatred and abuse. Many may not know this, but the worst kind of abuse is not physical but mental. I have been through seven years of mental torture by a man that pretended to love me but really didn't clearly love himself or anyone else. In order to love someone else, you first must love yourself.

Women need to learn how to empower other women and not stomp on each other over a man. There are those women who can see when a man has clearly lied to them about his status and is able to tell him to take the high road. However, many women like to give men the satisfaction of seeing them fight each other over him. In my story, you will see where I never fought any of these women, but I did confront them. This is wrong because the problem is never the other woman but the man that you're with. My story is filled with betrayal from other women who were trying to prove that this man was theirs, as well as his manipulation of these women.

For those of you who may never understand what a narcissist looks like, let me tell you. A narcissist creates a false persona. They will make you believe that they can give you the moon out of the sky. They make you believe that they are the friendly type. A narcissist preys on the insecure ones and the ones that do not value themselves, the ones that have a lot of self-hatred and self-esteem problems. This was me for some time until I found myself. They make you think that they are so easygoing, and nothing you can ever do will bother them. Being in love with a narcissist, you will think you hit the motherload; you will feel like a millionaire. A narcissist can make you believe that you are the one that is wrong, and they can do no wrong.

Below all that charm, humor, and self-confidence is a person who is selfish, manipulative, needy, and controlling. A narcissist does not believe that they are the ones with the problem, but the world and the people that they deal with are the ones with issues. When a person truly gets to know a narcissist, they will see that he is just a user and an abuser who is an angry, defensive, hostile individual. A narcissist is more looking for that one individual who they know they can manipulate, control, and make believe everything that he is saying as if it's the word of God.

My narcissist was always turning everything around to make it seem as if I were the one with the problem. He has manipulated his ex for so long into believing she would eventually be the one that she was willing to come into another woman's house to prove her loyalty to her controller. She even went as far as corrupting their daughter's mind to the point where his daughter believed every lie he ever told.

Women need to break free of the stereotype that they cannot coexist because they used to be with the same man. Instead of stooping to that level, women need to learn to encourage each other, if not for this generation, then for the generation to come. We need to lead by example for our younger generation.

2
THE BEGINNING

When she met him, she thought he was her world, her rock, her everything. The first day she walked around the corner and spotted him, she was taken in by his smooth appearance, and his calm, cool, collected demeanor. Nothing anyone could have said to her about him would have mattered. As she walked up to where he was sitting, she asked her friend about this fine specimen he was speaking to.

"Hey, Jah Jah? Who is your friend?"

To which he replied, "Why don't you ask him and find out?"

That afternoon, as she was going about her business, he approached her and said, "Hi! My name is Jessie. I would like to get to know you. Can I have your number?"

Playing hard to get and guarding her heart so as not to get hurt by yet another fast-talking handsome man, she kindly declined. Her mouth said no but her eyes said yes. He kept trying all afternoon until finally she gave in and gave him the number. That young woman was...*me.*

I met Jessie in 2009 when I had decided that I had given up on men and on love because of the games some men play on good women that destroys their self-esteem. He was a charming young man who I thought was my king. I worshipped him. I did anything he asked me to and believed anything that he told me. When I first met him, he introduced me to his son and told me he had one other child, but as our relationship grew, I started realizing that it was a lie. I learned of his other children from his wife at the time and mother. Yes, I said wife. When I met him, I did not know he was married, and I was always asking him every time we talked on the phone if he were sure he was single because it was hard to believe that a handsome man like him was still single.

When Jessie left the island that week we met, we had settled on moving to Georgia to start a family. While I stayed behind in the islands and continue to work, he was finding a place for us to live in Georgia. The time finally arrive for me to join my man in Georgia to build our family like we previously discussed. However, as if the heavens were speaking to me, I started recognizing a change in him but decided to overlook it all in the name of love.

We spent about four years in Georgia before he made the decision that we needed to move halfway across the country for a fresh start. While in Georgia for those four years, I found out that he was cheating with more women than I could count. I left him twice but always came back because I thought the problem was me and if I just changed, maybe he wouldn't cheat anymore. Sad mistake that was. Closing my eyes to things and acting as if the late nights into early mornings didn't bother me seemed to give him cause to continue to do as he pleased and disrespect me. I didn't help the situation because I was always searching, digging, recording, and looking for anything to start an argument about his infidelity. Finally, I decided to just give him more and do more for him to show him that I loved him so things might get better. I set dates and created trips just to save my relationship. I hoped that my fiancé would see just how much I loved him. It worked for a while, and we moved to New Jersey to start over. Well, he moved a month before I did only because I was eight months pregnant with our son. February 2014 came, and it was time to say goodbye to Georgia. Hello, New Jersey. Hello, new life. WRONG.

It was the first day in New Jersey when I overheard his conversation with another woman. I already knew that while he was supposed to be securing a place for our future to start over with each other, he was busy romancing someone else. Things went from bad to worse in New

Jersey because not only was I being ignored; I was being lied to even more often than before. This was because he needed to cut his time between me and someone else. His aunt came into town for a visit, and while I was trying to set things up and be a gracious host, he was busy making plans to introduce his aunt to his new side piece.

That summer, my uncle came for a visit, and he made my uncle's visit and my life a living hell by claiming that my uncle was not my uncle but in fact another man I was sleeping with. This is the second time I had enough and decided it was time for me to get away from him and his madness before I either killed him or killed myself. I felt like I was going insane dealing with his gaslighting, manipulations, and accusations because he was sleeping around and claiming these women were either nobody or a friend.

His charm, his smooth talking, and his promise once again of a bright future for us and the children was drawing me back in. However, I decided that I wasn't going to be sucked back in so easily; I was going to make him prove to me how much the children and I really meant to him.

Remember how I mentioned in the beginning that I found out about his other children from his wife? Yes! This man was married, and I had no idea that he was. His wife called me up when I first met him and told me to stay away from her husband. When I called him on it, he claimed she was not his wife and she was just a baby mama. After that, I did make it clear that I wanted to just be friends because I was not going to put 100 percent of my trust into another man only to be crushed to pieces again. To prove to me that he wanted me and the children, he filed for divorce from his wife. Now I know a lot of people are going to judge and say, "Wait. She's talking about him and his cheating, yet she was sleeping with him the whole time he was married."

Let me put all of that to rest right now. What I learned from the attorney that was doing his immigration paperwork was that he originally got married for the papers and that his own wife at the time said so. I know. I know. That is still no excuse for dating a married man. I know this was wrong, no matter the circumstance or manner under which they were married. *They were still married.* However, can anybody truly say they know 100 percent about the person they are or were dating from day one? No! Yes, I found out weeks after he and I started dating that he was married, and I made it clear to him that we couldn't be together, even though it was made clear to me that he got married for papers.

3
CHANGES AND NEW BEGINNINGS . . .OR ARE THEY?

After receiving confirmation that he was divorced and he moved hundreds of miles closer to where I was staying, I believed the man I met in the beginning was ready to stop playing games and settle down. They say home is where the heart is, and sometimes to fix a problem you have to go home to get some wisdom. In 2015, we decided to travel back to the islands because of some issues he was having that needed to be fixed and could only be done back home. Going home did help fix his issues but created issues for me because of his guilt, insecurity, and jealousy. Everything was great when we got back to the islands. Oh no! Wait! It wasn't.

On the first day back, I realized his phone would ring, and he would ignore it. I already knew him, so I knew something wasn't right. Once again, I chose to ignore it for the sake of saving my relationship. I pretended for months that I didn't notice the young woman that kept calling and leaving messages. I pretended for months that I didn't notice the late-night light of the phone as this woman and yet another woman would call all hours of the night, trying to get in touch with him. I decided to continue working on building my relationship and not letting my anger get the best of me because, believe me, I am not the one to mess with or get angry.

He proposed to me three times. The first time, I turned him down after saying yes because of the infidelity and lies, and felt he wasn't ready. The second time, I never gave an answer, but the third time, even though that small voice told me not to do it, I said yes. I figured if he kept asking, he must be serious!

The islands are so tropical and very good for beach weddings and church weddings. I have always wanted a church wedding with all the bells and whistles just so I can feel like a princess on my special day. However, when he said he wanted a court wedding, I did not fight it; I just agreed. That's not how our wedding turned out, and it was only because of this woman that acted like my second mother. She encouraged him to think of a church wedding, and he agreed.

What made me further overlook my husband's infidelity and tell myself that he truly loved me, even if he didn't act like it was, he decided to start attending church with me. In all my years of knowing him, I could never get him to say yes to going to church with me. He fit right in nicely with our church family. He was such a big help in fixing up the church, getting the lights done and helping me with the technology in the church. One Sunday, we took it upon ourselves to speak to the pastor about counseling before we took that step down the aisle. Jessie is a sweet talker, and he can sell ice to an Eskimo. He had a way of making anyone believe that he was a genuinely nice, caring, loving husband and father. Believe me, it worked because even my own father liked him for me and had encouraged me to settle down with him. This was until the day he said something to my father just a few short days before our wedding that made my father change his mind. But it was already too late because thousands of dollars would have been wasted.

Being back home was great, but as usual, when he felt trapped or intimidated by another man—whether it is my uncle, my brother or my cousin, or even my friends—he wanted to up and run so that he could take me away from my support system and the people that would be there for me. Was it all done out of jealousy or was it all done out of guilt? That is the million-dollar question. While he was looking for jobs so we could uproot our family once again over things that made no sense, I had this terrible gut feeling like we were rushing out of the islands before our time. But hey, I was his wife now, and I had to follow.

The transition back to the States was not hard. It was what happened after we transitioned that was hard. It's like when we landed in Louisiana, he just decided to pick up from where he left off when we left the States in 2015. At this time, I had already taken his daughter into my house because I cared for her like my own and just wanted to help create a bright future for her. The events that followed led me to realize I was being used and manipulated by a child who was being used and manipulated by her mother, but what transpired was all on ME. No other woman would bring another woman into their house, especially if the woman is an ex of their man/husband. I, on the other hand, did not think that way because I wanted to break that stereotype of two women fighting over one man under the same roof.

4
THE BETRAYAL

Jessie was always looking for a reason to leave or to say that I was the one cheating on him all along. Back in New Jersey, he claimed my uncle was not my uncle and was indeed a man I was sexually entangled with behind his back. Why? *Because he never met my uncle before.* Back in the islands, the same thing happened again. While we were working on the church, my cousin and I were accused of having an affair with each other because we were both on our phones at the same time. Remember that daughter I spoke about? Well, when we arrived in Louisiana, I realized she was just as manipulative as her dad but, I never said anything. To me, I was her stepmother, and all I could do was try to tell her about some the things I've been through and hope she would learn from my struggles and my mistakes and not let any man run over her.

One thing I realized about his daughter was how very materialistic she was and how when you told her no, she seemed to catch an attitude. I never understood why until those fateful two months her mother came for a visit. I've always heard the saying that men cheat because they think they can, but women cheat when they are not getting any love and attention at home. Let me tell you, that is so true because you have no idea how many times, I've wished someone would show me some love and affection so I could leave this man. Now don't get me wrong. That's not to say that there aren't some women out there that just cheat for cheating sake, because there are. There was a neighbor, Jack, the same neighbor Tammy claimed I slept. He would talk to Tammy about life and about some of the things he saw on the streets. He did this because he too saw the way she behaved and dressed daily. He tried to educate her on being a lady, something her own father refused to do. Tammy also claimed I slept with the pastor of our church and went on dates. The pastor who was kind enough to either pick us up and drop us back off on Sundays or have his wife pick us up and drop us off, she lied on as well. Mm mm, how low can one person be to make up such frivolous lies to get what they want.

Back to the situation regarding Jack. Being neighbors, we would all sit and talk about life, the problems the world was facing. One day the neighbor's son as well as Jack happen to mention they didn't like the fact that this man I'm married to was sleeping out and coming in at mornings. When I confronted Jessie one day and told him how embarrassing it was what he was doing, he said to me,

"I'm a grown-ass man. I can do what I want."

I used to say to him, "No, Jessie. You're a grown-ass married man who should bring his ass home at nights instead of sleeping in every chick's bed who says, 'Oh you have sexy lips or eyes.'"

One day, while we were all sitting around talking, Jack saw my face and pulled me aside to talk. In our conversation he told me a story about his mother and father. He was also encouraging me to stick it out until I knew I had enough, and it was time for me to move on.

He said to me, "My father used to cheat on my mother constantly, but she stuck by him regardless. Now I'm not saying you should keep taking that kind of abuse and disrespect, but don't throw away your relationship if you're not sure that is what he's doing. And, if, that is what you know 100 percent that he is doing, then you must be the one to decide when enough is enough. My mother stayed married to my father for twenty-five years until the day he died. Yes, I've seen my mother miserable most days because she knew where my father was when he didn't come home, but she never let his infidelity and disrespect break her spirit. You are a beautiful woman who can get any man. You have to be the one to change your situation."

I respected Jack because, while he was showing me that he listens, and that he genuinely cares, I was drawn to him and secretly wishing *he* was my husband. However, I was grateful he was just a friendly neighbor.

I tried to give Tammy just the things she needed and not what she wanted, but that was never enough for her and I later found out why. Jessie's ex, Tammy's mother, Evelyn, and I had a great relationship, or so I thought. She was the one out of all the women he had been with that I got along with. However, I found out the two months that she was in my house neither her nor her daughter ever liked me. They were just using me to get close to me so they could exact their revenge on him and the women they think took him from them. However, like I said, Jessie is a sweet talker and a manipulator and apparently, he still had control over her and her daughter. They went from trying to hurt him, to him convincing them, that *I* was their problem.

The day Tammy's mother called her daughter up and said she wanted to visit; I had no problems with that at all. I believe in women empowering women. I believe two women can coexist under the same roof, if they both strong enough, with no issues whatsoever. But I guess I was a bigger woman for thinking that. Jack, the same man that his Tammy claimed I slept with, spoke to me once again in a mature manner. He asked me where Evelyn was staying, and I told him in my house. This is when you know you have a great man talking to you.

He sat me down, and he said to me, "I know you want to be nice, and I know you want to help your stepdaughter to see her mother, but do not let that woman stay in your house."

I responded, "No, no. It's fine. She and I are cool, and we have been through the same things with the same man, so you have nothing to worry about. I know you care for me, but it's fine. Really."

Three weeks after speaking those words to him, I started noticing a change in her every time I walked into my own house. What did I do? NOTHING.

I realized every time I walked into my house, with Jessie at home, she was always bringing up the times they were together. I also saw that they would sit and speak in their native tongue, talking bad about my daughter. She thinks her child is better than anyone else and even went as far as telling him, her daughter was his only child. What stung the most was when I was speaking to his daughter, she started acting like she didn't hear me and refused to answer.

September 26, 2017 was the day Jessie, his daughter, and his ex, decided to kill my joy and my spirit and break me into a million pieces.

It was the same day he left to take a job I specifically told him not to take because of a dream I had about that job. I told Jessie about the dream I had of him getting into a fight with his boss over him constantly being late.

I told him, "Jessie baby if you take this job you will lose it within matter of months. Remember you and Roger never got along when we worked at the Marriott. He's not as good as you. To him you're intimidating and that alone is going to cause conflict. He is going to find a reason to get rid of you."

Yet, Jessie took the job on the advice of another woman who came into my house, took my kindness for weakness, and smiled in my face while her daughter threw daggers at my back. A twenty-year-old, who acts like a two-year old, that I loved dearly, stabbed me so deep over material things. All to help her mother exact revenge on a man who left her sixteen years ago, without caring who she hurt in the process. She claimed I was sleeping with Jack because she saw him give me a hug and a kiss on the cheek while comforting me one day.

I don't know about anyone else, but if I were going to cheat on my husband, I would not be stupid enough to walk with his twenty-year-old daughter. She is old enough and very capable of watching the younger ones. I would find a reason to leave the house just so I can go get me some temporary happiness. However, everywhere I went, they ALL, including his twenty-year-old child, was always, ALWAYS with me. I never went anywhere without my children, and by my children, I meant his child as well. As, long as Jessie and I have been together, he never once genuinely came out and said, "Let me take my wife out." But because a friend decided he wanted to take me and kids to show us Louisiana, his daughter claimed I went on dates with this man.

Even after everything Evelyn and her daughter, Tammy, put me through, when my husband left Louisiana, he left his daughter and this woman in my house for me to continue being a gracious host to. Being the kind of person and the woman that I am, I still showed those two utmost love and kindness. Jessie called every day after he left and never asked to speak to me, *his wife*. Instead, he asked to speak to this woman *every single day* he called. She talked in their native tongue on the phone to *my* husband, bashing me, and then got off the phone and smiled oh-so-sweetly like she and I were the best of friends. See I've been with Jessie long enough to pick up some things that he says in Creole, so I picked up some of what he was saying by her responses. His daughter, on the other hand, would parade herself around like she won the lottery because to her she had destroyed me and made me miserable. What hurt me the most was that I was never ever mean or wicked to this child. I treated her like she was mine. To make matters worse, when Evelyn was leaving to go back home, she, her daughter, and Jessie concocted a plan to make me broke and trapped on the streets of New Orleans. But God had a different plan in mind. The day they all left Louisiana and left me half broke, I felt like minute shards that no one could possibly put back together. BUT GOD…oh God…if it was not for Him, looking out for me always, I would have never made it to Georgia.

5
SAVED BY TRAGEDY

<u>BEFORE THE FIRE</u>

After about a year of being apart, when I was finally getting myself together, Jessie decided he wanted his family back. He texted me and said he wanted to talk about working things out and being a family again. Everything inside me screamed "big mistake." However, I thought about his request for weeks before I decided to call him to let him know what my demands were.

Ring. Ring. Ring. No answer. "Maybe he is busy." I knew he worked two jobs, so I was not going to sweat it. That's what I was telling myself in my head. After about five rings, I decided to leave a message.

"Hey, Jessie. I wanted to talk to you about what you said the other day. Give me a call back when you get this message."

The next day, instead of calling, he texted me, "Hey! What's up?"

I said, "What's up is me wanting to talk to you about what you wanted because I have boundaries, and you have to meet those before I can commit to anything."

I didn't get much of a response after that, and I left it alone. From there, we would talk on and off concerning the kids and what we wanted for our future. There was something in me that just wouldn't let go of the fact that something still seemed off with him. After weeks of talking about what we wanted and what we were going to do differently this time around, I started noticing the same old disrespect.

One day, when I took the children to see him, I noticed he would constantly check his phone and turn it upside down. Now there are a couple reasons a person would turn his phone upside down. However, since I had been down this road with him before, I already knew why he did that. When there is another woman calling, he always had a habit of turning his phone upside down and ignoring the ringing. His phone rang again, and he ignored the call. It rang over and over that night like it was an emergency and this person just really needed to get in touch with him. There were the days when he would ignore my calls and texts, then give me excuses when he finally did reach back out to me.

Jessie always wanted to become a police officer, so I decided to help him with the process. As I was going through his email for correspondence form the recruiting officer, I noticed something. One day I really needed $40 extra to pay the daycare fee for our son, and I asked him for it. He had me wait all day before he finally answered, and of course had an excuse to go with it. However, in searching the email, I noticed that there was a Cash App amount for the $40 from Dionne Williams. Now I knew who Miss Williams was because she was the same young lady that he was sleeping with before we left Louisiana. Last I checked, Jessie claimed it was over with them, so I was flabbergasted. Why would Ms. Williams send him $40? I left it alone and went on with what I was doing. I told myself if it were anything, the lies would show themselves.

Two weeks later, our Junior broke his tablet, so I texted Jessie: "Hey, babe. JJ needs his tablet back."

"Okay" he replied, "I will get him another one tomorrow."

The next day, as I was going through the emails, replying to recruiters, in came a Cash App email. "Jessie London, you have received $60 for bed from Dionne Williams." Later that day, Jessie wanted the kids and I to come to his place because he claimed he had something for us. When I made it to his house that night, he had a tablet for Junior. I was furious, boiling inside, because I knew where he got the money from to purchase that tablet. I was more pissed because after all that talk of wanting to reconcile and stopping his cheating and changing his ways, it seemed that Jessie had not changed.

Weeks went by like that. I kept using his email to send correspondence back and forth, finding out what he would need to get this police course done, and always seeing these Cash App emails from Ms. Dionne Williams. I finally had enough of it the day when he was moving. The day of the move, he said he didn't have enough money to pay the deposit, so he was going to ask his boss for a loan. As we're riding towards his workplace, he was busy texting. By the time we got to his job, my phone vibrated. By this time, I had already attached his email to my phone to receive alerts, and it was a Cash App message. I finally had it by then, so I called him on it.

"Hey, Jessie. Tell me something. How are you going to tell me that you want to reconcile, but you're still having an affair with the same chick you were sleeping with before we left Louisiana?"

His response was, "What are you talking about? I'm not having an affair with anybody. I don't even talk to that girl."

To which I replied, "Oh, really? So, she just randomly sends you money every week in different amounts?"

He responded with yet another lie, "You need to stop listening to people. If a person does something and I don't know about it, I don't have any control over that."

With anger in my voice I replied, "Wait a minute. You must take me for a complete idiot, right? This is not only disrespectful to me, but it is also not fair to her as well. This girl has invested time and money into you, and you are constantly lying to her, to me, to both of us."

Within a matter of minutes of having that conversation, I received another ping. A Cash App email stated that the email would no longer be associated with the Cash App account. By this time, he was already out of the car and heading into his job. I just smiled and left it alone.

A couple weeks later, as I was sending some follow-up emails to the recruiter for Dekalb county, the email account closed out on me. Then I received a ping saying that the password was changed, the secondary email was changed, and the recovery telephone number for the email was changed. I immediately called him up.

He answered, "Hey, babe. What's up?"

With anger in my voice I said, "Don't what's up me, Jessie. How are you going to ask me to help you get into the police force, yet you give your email address to an individual you claim you are not still messing with?"

"What are you talking about?", he replied, "Nobody but you have my email address."

Still angry I replied, "Oh really. So, you are telling me that you didn't give Ms. Dionne your email address?"

"No". he stated, "What are you talking about?"

"Wow". sounding really surprised, "You must think I am really stupid, huh? I received a notification on my phone letting me know that the password was changed, and it was done close to Texas."

Jessie still being Jessie replied, "I don't know anybody in Texas."

"I know that dummy," I interjected, "but Louisiana is just but a distance from Texas. And, how do you explain her telephone number as the secondary number?"

"What number?", he said sounding all surprised.

"504-555-7652. Really? You going to play dumb with me? You cannot tell me that that isn't her number either, because you gave me her name as one of your references for your job application."

"Honestly, babe, I don't know whose number that is." he said with a smirk in his voice.

There was a picture I found in the iPhone he had me jailbreak so I said, "Okay. So, explain to me this picture that you have with her name and your last name attached with that same number." I sent him the same screen shot that he took, that showed, **My Queen Dee London 504-555-7652.**

There was complete silence for two weeks, and I couldn't care less.

Did it hurt me that he was still playing those childish games? Yes, it did. After that two weeks of nothing from him, Jessie had the audacity to ask me to delete the email address because he didn't like people in his business. I was a bit confused. He was the one that gave the email address to her, but because he was caught by both of us, I had to delete his email for him. Why? So, he can continue with his lies!

For a man who claimed he was done with the games, he sure loved to create drama. Jessie didn't have cable in his new place so I gave him the information to my Netflix and my Hulu accounts so he could be entertained. Two weeks after doing so, I noticed the names on my Hulu changed to that of his name; Dionne; and his daughter, Tammy. I took a picture and texted it to him and asked him what that was. No answer. Then I decided to check my Netflix just for the heck of it and same situation. That was the last straw for me. I tried calling and tried texting. No answer.

Finally, after two weeks of no calls and no texts, he texted me to ask me to bring the kids over because he missed us. I decided to take that time to confront him. As he opened the door and I stormed inside, the first question out of my mouth was: "Who the hell was here?" This man looked pass me and said, "Nobody". However, as I entered the bathroom, I noticed tampons, and I asked the question again. This was when he proceeded to tell me that his daughter was there for two weeks, and she was the one that changed my information.

"Jessie, this is the last straw. One of us has to go. You know I would never ask anyone to get rid of their child. But I am your wife, and I come before your daughter in this marriage. She is twenty-one and old enough to make something of her life. As long as I will be in your life, that child is not welcome in my house until she has some respect. I have been like a mother to her for seven years, loved her like my own and all I get from her is disrespect. I brought her here out of the kindness of my heart, and this is how you, she, and her mother has repaid me. All this is because of your lies and manipulation, and it stops today. Either she goes or I go."

Jessies responded, "But she is my daughter though."

After he said that, I left his place saying to myself, "Fine, sir. You have made your choice."

I reached out to Tammy and confronted her, told her she needed to mind her business and stay out of me and my husband's business. I told her instead of sticking her nose into marital affairs that does not concern her she needs to concentrate on her status in this country. I encouraged her to spend time thinking about herself and where she wants to be in life. I even went as far as to let her know I do not hate her, I pity her, because she allowed the love of material things to make the decisions that she did. This was the disrespectful reply I received:

"First off and let me say this perfectly clear: I do not live with you or your husband. I do not want anything else from you or your husband, nor would I ever need anything from you ever again. I work nine hours a day, seven days a week. I do not have time to be worrying about you. As for my status in this country, whether straight or bend, you do not have to worry. Plus, I already received my papers without your malicious intent in it. If you want to talk, we can do this in person."

I took care of this child for seven years from afar. I kept encouraging her father to look for her and stop chasing skirts. I made sure her education in Antigua was paid for, even when I was broke, and my own son was not receiving my support. I felt sorry for her being in Antigua when she could come to the states and get more opportunities, so I brought her here. This child had the balls to tell me that I had malicious intent toward her.

I replied and let her know I had no business meeting the devil or any of his minions anyplace After saying that to her, she replied with the nastiest disrespect one can ever get from a child they took care of and fought for.

"Bitch, you're scum. You're a bird. You're nobody. You're basic so go back to your basic life. Keep on fighting for a man that treats you like the piece of shit that you are."

All I had to say to that child after that was: "Thank you for those kind words." That was the day before the fire.

THE FIRE HAPPENED

I will never forget December 2, 2018. As I drove into the Polo Club subdivision, I noticed a big commotion outside. When I looked in the direction of the apartments, I noticed it was on fire. I drove as fast as I could around to the opposite end to find my children. As I drove up, I saw my children and my friend running down a flight of burning stairs. They were the last set of individuals to get out of the burning building. I watched in horror and amazement as my children ran down a stair that was on fire. I ran out of my car and immediately scooped them up.

A few minutes after securing my children I called Jessie first. After calling him for what felt like forever, he finally answered the phone: "Yeah."

"Jessie, the apartment is on fire," I sobbed.

"Hello." he replied, "I can't understand you"

I calmed myself down a bit so he could understand what I was saying. "Jessie, the apartment is on fire. We almost lost the kids, but they just made it out."

"Okay." he said, with no concern whatsoever in his voice.

After a pause, he said the most insensitive thing any man could ever say to his wife who just let him know she almost died, or a father could say after hearing he almost lost his children.:

"Let me know what happened, I'm tired. I worked two jobs so I'm going to bed."

I was in awe and already upset so I didn't have the strength to fight with him, so I just hung up the phone.

I immediately got on the other line and called my best friend of eleven years and told him what was happening.

"Hey Ryan", still sobbing, "the apartment is on fire, I've lost everything."

He asked, "where are you, where are the kids. Is everybody okay."

"We're at the complex still," I replied, "the ambulance is about to take the kids to Grady Memorial."

His instant reply was, "okay, I'm at a concert but I'll meet you at the hospital."

Twenty minutes after I reached Grady memorial, Ryan showed up. This man left a concert where he was with a friend to come make sure my children and I were okay, and my own husband told me he was too tired to come look for us. Not only did this man came to comfort me and my children, but he handed me the keys to his place and said, "You can stay there as long as you want or until you find a place because I am never there."

Days after the fire, when my son was finally out of the hospital, Jessie called to find out where I was. At this point, I didn't care what he thought, he couldn't guilt trip me anymore or make me feel bad about having friends or even accepting help from family and friends. So, I told him flat out: "I'm staying at my friend's house who came and looked for your family; something you didn't care to do."

For a long while, I didn't get a response from him. Hours later, while I was crying my eyes out and trying to process everything that just happened, this man texted me with his crap.

"Hey, I don't like the fact that my kids are at another man's house when I have a two-bedroom, furnished apartment. If you want to stay, you can stay, but bring me the kids."

At this point, I was boiling inside because he didn't care what happened to them, then he wants to pretend he cared because someone else did. And then he had the audacity to tell me to bring them, but I could stay. You see, I knew how this man thought. In his small peanut brain, he thought the only reason I was at this man's apartment was because he and I had something going on. Jessie may have been my husband, but he left me and these children on the streets of Louisiana and walked away. Due to that fact, my goings and comings or who I talk to, was none of his business. When we needed him the most, he chose to stay where he was and let us burn. He wanted to say to everyone he's been lying to, "See? I told y'all she was cheating. This is why I did what I did to her." This was when I decided to let him know he was wasting his time with his gaslighting because I was no longer the naïve woman he married. My eyes were wide open; my strength was back, and I had found my voice.

As the days went by, I was trying to figure where do I go from here, how I was going to get everything back, how was I going to buy food and still pay everything else while trying to rebuild my life. I took a week off to get my mind right and work on finding a place to live as well as cancel some bills. First thing I decided to do was cancel some accounts and put some on hold until I was able to pay for them because all my money will be going into buying food, commute, daycare and some clothes. As I was going through my Netflix and Hulu accounts once again to put them on hold, I realized once again that the names had changed. This man stooped very low again and changed the names on my Hulu and Netflix to his name, Dionne Williams, and his daughter's name. I shook my head and laughed, and said, "Thank you, Jesus." Right then is when I decided that this man was incapable of change, and it would have been a waste of time and more hurt if I had decided to reconcile with him. I went straight to the courthouse the next day and refiled the divorce paperwork once more.

Just like Shadrach, Meshach and Abednego, God protected my children and I through this fire. We came out unharmed, untouched, and with our sanity intact. Jesus held my hand through this whole ordeal and helped me to make the right choice for my children and me. I'm not talking about the physical fire; I am talking about the fire of putting myself and my children back in that man's life only to get hurt worse than before. I am thankful for the strength God gave me to make the right decision. I asked God for a sign, and he showed it to me like he was for seven years, but I never listened. This time the only difference is, I decided to start paying attention to the signs God was giving me.

6
EXPOSING MYSELF

In all my struggles dealing with Jessie and his infidelity, manipulation, and gaslighting, I was losing myself. There were days I felt like it was not worth living; depression was holding me tightly, and I did not want to get help. I was afraid of what people would say about me. When I finally decided to get help because I felt suicidal at times, Jessie basically laughed at my pain and called me crazy. I don't know if it was not wanting to fail my parents or if it was the hand of God, but I made it through.

Depression is not to be taken lightly. I was taking my depression lightly for all the wrong reasons. Finally, I decided to get some help to get my depression under control. But it was not enough. I was still spiraling out of control like I did not have a grip on life. I went to the Veteran's Affairs medical center and asked to speak with a mental health specialist who placed me on Prozac to control my mood. However, when I became pregnant with my youngest son, I decided to take myself off. During my pregnancy, everything seemed fine or so I would have liked to believe. No one should ever get pregnant to hold on to a man, and I know some of you might think that's what I did, but that is far from the truth. When I became pregnant with my son, I wanted to abort him, but God had a different answer for me.

After our son was born, I didn't expect Jessie to get any better, but I was hoping that he would. Things reached a point where I packed my things and left before the sun was up just to get away before I lost my mind or my life. Things were great until I made the sad mistake of going back to him. Once again, four years after I took myself off the antidepressants, I had to be placed back on them because I was so depressed, I felt like life was not worth living. I once again sought treatment from the Veteran's Affairs and talked things out with a therapist almost every week, but that still wasn't enough. I left every therapy session angrier than before I went, so my doctor increased the dosage and gave me some additional medication that would help. My mother and father taught me to always take my troubles to God in prayer, but I felt at the time like God was not listening. He had let me down.

When Tammy and her mother, Evelyn decided to be vindictive and try to kill my spirit, I almost let them, but I fell to my knees and prayed harder than I ever had. I let God know I couldn't do this without him, and I needed him to keep me strong because I felt extremely weak. It is said that God has an angel for everyone just right around the corner, my old boss at AutoZone told me that, and it is true. Just when my mind was trying to deceive me, play tricks on me, and make me believe I was not worthy, God sent more than one angel my way to let me know I could and would make it and he had a better life for me. First it was a Facebook post by Pastor Marcus Gill: that said, "God will remove certain people out of your life to make space for the right people to bless you". I then saw a video of Lisa Nichols sharing her story of poverty, abuse, and let downs. After speaking with Iyanla Vanzant's producer I went in search of her page and saw a couple of her inspirational and powerful speeches. All of these helped me to realize, God is not done with me yet and he is telling me I too can make it past these tough times.

I spent most my nights the first few months just crying my eyes out over how much my heart ached. I finally opened my eyes after my son saw me breaking down one night and said to me, "Aww, Mommy, don't cry. It's going to be okay.", I realized it was God speaking to me through my son that **everything was going to be okay.**

Stand for something or fall for anything. Today's mighty oak is yesterday's nut that held its ground."

Rosa Park[1]

---

[1] (Park, n.d.)

7
STAND FOR SOMETHING OR FALL FOR ANYTHING

When I was a teenager, I used to always hear my dad say, "Stand for something or you will fall for anything.", I never quite understood what that meant. As I grew older, I started to understand what it meant. I was the type of person that always wanted to do the right thing so people would like me, even if it meant holding my tongue when I knew something was not right.

Before bringing Evelyn into my house, all the signs were there. My own stepmother told me she felt something in her spirit. I also had a recurring dream of a snake trying to suffocate me. However, because I wanted this woman to see that I would do anything for her child and longed for her to appreciate me for doing my best, I allowed her to come in and further corrupt my house. Did I stand up for me? No, I didn't. I allowed everything to happen that shouldn't have. Tony Blair said it best when he said: "Sometimes it is better to lose and do the right thing than to win and do the wrong thing." If only I had just said no to that woman coming into my house, things would have ended, *yes*, but it would have ended differently. It would have ended on my terms.

After all the betrayal and hurt, when Jessie decided he finally wanted his family back but still wouldn't change, I had to hold my ground. I didn't know how I was going to do it, but I decided to stay grounded. Friedrich Nietzsche said, "He who has a why to live for can hear almost any how."[2]

I had a why to live for. I had a purpose, and I knew it was not going to happen with me always choosing to overlook things and allowing people to treat me how they feel. In this life, you cannot be nice to everyone because not everyone knows how to handle kindness or others being nice to them. You cannot please everybody nor should you have to please everybody. You just have to live your life. People are always going to talk, whether you do good or whether you do bad. You have to be the one to say, "Do I care what others think or do I care what God thinks?"

We must recognize that no one can invalidate us. No one can make us feel less than we are. Looking to others for their validation is like handing them the reigns and have them ride you like a horse. In doing this, they will step all over you, and you will only have yourself to blame because you never stood your ground. None of us should never give anyone that much power.

Here is a scenario. What do you think would happen if God were to

---

[2] (Nietzsche, n.d.)

let Satan have his way and let him control us all? What do you think would happen? There would be nothing but chaos and destruction, and there would be no good in this world. This is what giving people your power does to your life. It makes you feel like you are never in control of your life. Stay true to yourself and always stand up for what you believe in. Never let anyone take advantage of your kindness or tell you that you cannot do something because it shows they are just afraid of the greatness within you.

"To change your reality, you must change your mentality."

Daniel Ally[3]

---

[3] (Ally, 2019)

8
CHANGE YOUR MENTALITY

Maybe if I stopped being friendly to others, my life with him would have been better. Maybe I need to lose some weight so I can look like what he wants. Maybe if I dress like half these females out here, I would be appealing to him. Maybe I am the problem. Maybe just by having friends, I really am cheating on him. Maybe I'm just not good enough for him. Maybe if I just let him do him and cheat with whomever he wants, things will be better. Maybe I should give up friends and family so that things will be better. Maybe I do not need to talk to anyone at all; maybe that would make him happy. Ever had these self-destructive thoughts run through your head? I have had all those thoughts and more.

The Bible says wives are to be submissive to their husbands, but there is no place in the Bible that says you must be blind and stupid. In order to live a healthy and drama-free life, you have to change your way of thinking, the way you approach things, and your mentality. Sometimes bad things happen in our lives because of the beliefs that we have held on to for so long. I used to believe that if I did not question, did not nag, and kept my mouth shut, my life would be so much better. **Wrong.**

Like I said even though the husband is the head doesn't mean the wife should act dumb. This all goes back to stand for something or fall for anything. If you are in a relationship with someone and you see them cheating or become abusive, keeping your mouth shut is not going to guarantee that your life won't be hell. In a relationship, you both should be held at an equal standard. Yes, do not emasculate him; let him wear the pants; let him be the head while you are his body. However, the only way for two hands to make a clapping sound is if they both move in unison and come together as one to make that sound. Bottling things up can only do more harm than good. One thing you should not have in your relationship with yourself or anyone else is FEAR. You can choose to live the life you want despite what fear says because fear is nothing but the work of the devil.

Think of it this way. If you commit a crime and you were caught and locked away for years, whose fault is that? Yours or society's? You can't blame society for your actions. When you create your own prison in life, the only person who can get you out of it is you. You are the only person that has the key to your own success with the help of God. Forget about anything negative that is holding you back and replace those thoughts with positive ones. How can one come about this change? By turning around and seeing a different side of things and liberating oneself from that prison of self-destruction, self-loathing, self-hatred, negative beliefs, bad habits, and anything else you can think of that you always use to do because of what you believed. We define our own truth. We create our own path. Choose to believe that your hurt won't last forever. Choose to believe that whatever you may have gone through in life was just for a time and a season, and it will all pass away. Hang on to the belief that you are worthy, blessed, enough, and loved. You are everything that the master created you to be. When you aren't given the truth from other people, remember he who holds our truth, Jesus Christ. He is the only one that can tell us we aren't worthy, and he would never do that.

In order to change your life, change the belief that everything you've heard about you that is NOT TRUE, *is not your truth*. You have the pen to draw your own image, so draw carefully and create the best portrait of yourself.

9
MENDING MYSELF

In mending myself, there were some steps that I followed, after burying myself for two months listening to Lisa Nichols encouraging story, I decided it was time I mended my broken self.

First, I decided it was time I Showed my scars. After sulking for what seemed like forever, I decided it was time I pull myself together. I decided instead of being afraid of what people would say because this man decided to use me then leave me, I was going to show myself some self-love.

Then I decided it was time for me to repair my brokenness. I started meditating just to ease the pressure off my mind and the pain out of my heart. I practiced a lot of self-love every day, started exercising with my brother, got involved in women's group, to keep my mind occupied.

In order to properly heal, we must learn to forgive ourselves and forgive our abusers. Forgiving my abusers was the hardest thing I had to do on my journey of self-discovery. I realized forgiveness is not for Jessie, Tammy or Evelyn, it was for me, and that is something that took me a long time to realize.

1. Was grateful for it all. I woke up giving God thanks for the things that was done and was very grateful that I was able to escape with my life.

2. Was a beacon of hope and light. I realize that there are also other women, and some men, out there that may be going through the same thing, or worse, that may need some encouragement. So, I decided to share my story and how I pulled through in hopes it would help someone else make that bold decision to give themselves a chance. I created the "Love Yourself Foundation" Facebook page.

3. Let my beauty shine. Sometimes situations can change people, but I have decided not to let this situation turn me into a monster, but a healer, a lover, and a fighter. I would not let the actions of others make me a monster just like them.

I read this piece on a Japanese art call Kintsukuroi, which is the art of repairing broken pottery using gold. It is their idea that a broken piece that is mended with gold is even more beautiful for having been broken. C. JoyBell states:

"In this life, we reap the results of everything that we do; even if the things that we do and the things that we become, are the direct results of circumstances that we could have never controlled, in the first place. They say we are never given more than we can handle; but I don't believe that. We are often given more than we can handle, and that's why so many of us are so broken. The jar breaks when there's too much to handle. The only beauty in all of this, is that jars can be repaired with gold; and because of that, they can become even more beautiful than they were before."[4]

Japanese people believe that we should turn our brokenness into beauty, strength, and wisdom and wear our brokenness and our scars proudly. We are human, and just like any object, we ourselves are fragile. We can never escape our brokenness because we're always going to have trials and tribulations during our time on this earth. Troubles that are meant to break us can also open our hearts. God uses the brokenhearted to bring the people that really need him close to him. We, as humans, are prone to great sorrows, but we are also destined for breathtaking joys. If we have never suffered, we may never know the beauty of what life holds for us or what God desires for us to be. If we never lose someone in this life, we can never know the great love that is out there for us. Being betrayed, lied to, lied on, mistreated,

---

[4] (JoyBell, 2015)

and abused is the key to our beauty. It took me a long time to realize my beauty didn't just lie in my looks, but what I radiate from my inner self. I had to realize that my brokenness is what made me the person I am today.

I decided that gold symbolized God's word and God's appearance in my life. I realized that if God did not know my strength, he would have never used those same people to break me into pieces until I was unrecognizable. But God is the only physician who can fully heal a broken heart, and he has never failed in his ability to heal. I remember singing a song in Sunday school that goes:

"Turn your eyes upon Jesus,

Look full in his wonderful face

And the things of earth will grow strangely dim

In the light of his glory and grace." [5]

Though our pain is real, and suffering is great, I've learned through my pain that God is always greater. **"He will not leave you or forsake you." (Deuteronomy 31:6)** There is this piece that I found that says, "You become more authentic because of your vulnerability, and you

---

[5] (Jackson, 2006)

are more empathetic because of your suffering." I know this to be true. I could have lost myself, been bitter, and treated everyone like the scum of the earth, but I didn't let my husband's infidelity or his daughter's betrayal change the person I was before all this. Even though I may guard myself from people, I try not to put every man, woman or child in the same bracket because of one bad experience, and I still try to love as much as I can. According to 1 Corinthians 13:12, the greatest weapon or gift you can have out of faith, hope and love is . . . LOVE. I allowed myself to feel broken for as long as my soul would allow me without losing myself, and then I picked myself up and decided to give life and love another chance. I was beautiful before I was broken, and I see myself as even more beautiful for having worked on my healing by starting with prayer and meditation before I could learn to forgive.

"Prayer is when you talk to God. Meditation is when God talks to you."

-Diana Robinson[6]

---

[6] (Robinson, n.d.)

10
PRAYER AND MEDITATION

Every morning I wake up, I give God thanks for it all: the hurt, the pain, the betrayal, and the heartache. As my feet hit the ground every single morning since that fateful day Jessie left, I say, "Thank you, Jesus, for this another day." I say that because I am still alive despite it all. After months of beating myself up, I returned to what I did before I started wallowing in self-pity. I pour myself into a different devotional each week. These devotionals were always centered around me loving myself, putting God first, coping with betrayal, living after a heartache as well as after a divorce. I read the Bible faithfully every morning and prayed for my healing.

Prayer should always be a part of our lives, whether you're a Christian or not. Prayer connects us with God spiritually and unites us with the holy spirit. My bedroom has two closets and since it's just me, I made one section as my prayer closet where I can sit in silence and have that one-and-one connection with God. I write out little prayers and stick them in the back of my closet, or I write them in a journal. When we sit in silence, we're able to have that connection so we can be filled with his Holy Spirit. Meditation and Prayer goes hand in hand. In order to be able to sit before God and pray what's truly on your heart, you have to find your center, relax, and just speak to God in a clear and focused manner.

When I first started meditating, it was hard because my thoughts were running wild. I couldn't relax no matter how hard I tried. As the weeks went by, I learned to meditate in quiet and with soft, soothing jazz music that helped to open my mind and take me away from my problems. The serenity prayer was one I recited daily for weeks on end to try and convince myself of the strength God has given me. Not the simple version but the full version of it.

"God grant me the serenity

To accept the things, I cannot change;

Courage to change the things I can;

And wisdom to know the difference.

Living one day at a time;

Enjoying one moment at a time;

Accepting hardships as the pathway to peace;

Taking, as he did, this sinful world

As it is, not as I would have it;

Trusting that He will make all things right

If I surrender to His Will'

So that I may be reasonably happy in this life

And supremely happy with Him

Forever and ever in the next.

Amen." [7]

The serenity prayer breathed life into me because it represented everything, I was seeking happiness, joy, and freedom from the evils of this world. I first had to accept that trials and tribulations are not here to break us, but to make us strong and propel us into what God has for us. The serenity prayer meditation was the most powerful meditation I came across. I started speaking God's favor towards me over my own life. **Jeremiah 29:11 (KJV) states; "For I know the plans I have for you declares the Lord, Plans to Prosper you and not to harm you, Plans to give you hope and a Future."** I started praying for not just my healing, but for forgiveness of the ones that tried to break me, the ones that betrayed me, and the ones that used me. Jesus said, **"Love your enemies and pray for those who persecute you,"** Matthew **5:44 (ESV).** He also said, **"Do good to those who hate you, bless those who curse you, pray for those who abuse you."** Luke 6:27-

[7] (Niebuhr, n.d.)

28 (ESV)

There were some days I did not feel like doing anything. In my healing process I realized perseverance was a must have on my journey to complete healing. It means me getting up every morning, pulling myself together and get out and conquer the day even if that is not how I feel. It was me trusting in God and know that he has a purpose for me. I tell myself if I can make it through my grief and pain, then I can make it through anything and I will come out the other end with a great reward, for pushing through even when I didn't feel like pushing.

In the beginning of my prayer and meditation life when I was trying to find peace within myself and with what was done, I would tell myself I forgave my adversaries. I didn't so I couldn't truly pray for them. I had to silently pray and ask God to teach me how to forgive so I knew how to effectively pray for the ones who persecuted me. Forgiveness doesn't happen overnight, but when you truly learn to forgive someone, that is when you will know how to truly pray for them in order to heal yourself.

"As I walked out the door toward the gate that would lead to my freedom, I knew if I didn't leave my bitterness and hatred behind, I'd still be in prison."

- Nelson Mandela[8]

---

[8] (Mandela, 2011)

11
FORGIVE THEM FOR YOU

Forgiveness is not for the abuser; it is for me to save my soul from becoming bitter and from eternal damnation. Jesus Christ didn't have to die on the cross for us, but he did. He forgave me even when I didn't deserve his forgiveness. He died for me, even when I didn't deserve such a sacrifice, so who am I to hold on to a grudge and not forgive my oppressors? My pastor from California once said to me when I was going through a tough time in my first marriage, "write down the pros and cons about your husband. If the pros outweigh the cons, then you know you can work things out but if the cons outweigh the pros then you know what you need to do. I heard something like this recently, about one's wrongdoings, that if it serves no purpose in your life let it go, do not dwell on the wrongdoings.

It took me awhile to understand what that meant, and as I kept thinking about the wrong that was done to me, I never could get through halfway without anger and bitterness creeping up into my soul. It had taken me months to realize I was getting angry for no reason because it already happened, and it was bound to so why get angry *again*. I have since trashed my list, but sometimes, when I think of it, I laugh at myself for being so silly to think that mere words on a paper of the wrongdoings could still hurt me. I prayed so much for God to help me in my forgiveness process that if I were God, I would ask me why I was still asking when he had already given me the tools to forgive and have already answered my prayer.

In the beginning, when I convinced myself I had forgiven them, I did not. Let me explain that for those of you who may not understand what I mean. One can say they forgive someone or tell themselves that they do, but deep down, they still hold a grudge and secretly wish the worst for their abusers. That was me in the beginning, I was secretly wishing they all would get what they deserve. When my husband lost the same job, I told him not to take, I was secretly rejoicing that that happened to him while I was helping him find another job and pretending, I wasn't happy he didn't have one. When immigration denied his daughter's paperwork, even though I told myself I wasn't happy about it, I secretly was. I decided to truly pray and ask God to help me in my healing process and turn my attention from my abusers and the pain they caused me because that pain was meant for my good. In reading my prayer journal, I came across a forgiveness prayer that I have read multiple times and even circled because I so desperately needed God's help in learning to forgive my husband and my stepdaughter. It reads:

"Lord, you know the people I struggle to forgive. It feels impossible to let go of how they've hurt me. But in Christ you forgave me for everything I've done, and you call your children to follow your example. Help me forgive them, Lord—as many times as it takes." [9]

Not only was I praying for the Lord to help me forgive them and move on, but also for him to forgive me for my actions or thoughts toward them because of what they did. In order to heal, you can ask God to forgive you as well, and this is how you do so:

"Jesus, your forgiveness is such a beautiful gift! No matter what it is or how many times I've struggled when I confess, you take the burden off my shoulders; the sin I carried is gone. Thank you for inviting me to confess and for promising that I will always find forgiveness in you."

In praying for your forgiveness and others as well, you start to heal not

---

[9] (Dahl Silver, 2019)

just your heart, but your soul, and then you can move on.

Lewis B. Smedes says, "To forgive is to set a prisoner free and discover that the prisoner was you."[10] I was holding myself prisoner to my abusers by constantly hoping and wishing they would hurt as much as I was hurting instead of truly forgiving them for what they did. Now don't get me wrong; nobody said you must forget what was done to you, but you must forgive in order to truly heal.

Forgiveness was the second step in truly healing my brokenness, and it has helped me to grow into a stronger person. After forgiving my abusers and setting myself free, I started feeling grateful for the things that was done to make me stronger, not weaker.

---

[10] (Smedes, 1997)

"Take life day by day and be grateful for the little things. Don't get caught up in what you can't control. Focus on the positive."

Unknown[11]

---

[11] (Unknown, 2016)

12
BE GRATEFUL FOR EVERYTHING

Whether good or bad, no matter what happens to us in this lifetime, we need to always be grateful because God never gives us more than we can handle. **Psalms 91:1-2 (KJV) reads, "He that dwelleth in the secret place of the most high shall abide under the shadow of the almighty. I will say of the Lord, he is my refuge and my fortress, my God in him I will trust."** In order to be grateful for what God has done in our lives, we first have to **trust** that God knows what he is doing for our lives. Without trust in God, one cannot know what gratefulness looks or feels like. Our tears and pain were never an original part of God's plan for our lives, nor will we have to endure them in the thereafter. Suffering is only for a time. It will not always last, and our suffering is also due to the choices that we make.

I stand in my mirror every morning and give God thanks for blessing me with another beautiful day. I tell myself how grateful I am that I still have breath. I look at myself and let me know just how much I love her. I look deep into my soul to see my scars. I look at myself and see the verbal self-infliction, and I just let it all out and give God thanks for it all. God does not manufacture pain; he uses our pain and put it to good use to help us be a better version of ourselves. The truth of the matter is that we just need to have a little faith, never give up, and always give God thanks for everything in this life, good or bad. **Romans 8:28 (KJV) says, ". . . and we know that all things work together for good for them that love God, to them who are the called according to his purpose."** I learned that what happened to me almost a year ago was meant to happen. It was part of God's plan to get me to the place he wants me to be.

In the face of adversities, we have to learn how to be grateful. David was a mere boy when he fought Goliath, and even though nobody believed he could win, he stood against that giant and trusted God to get him through that ordeal. He was grateful for the opportunity to be used as a vessel to protect his people and had faith that he would get it done.

Joseph took more than what God intended him to bare. He had cause to be ungrateful after his own brothers sold him into slavery, but instead, he was humble and gave God thanks for all he went through. He was abandoned, enslaved, betrayed, and estranged yet he was grateful for it all. Job lost everything but was still grateful to God for everything. Even when his own friends wanted him to give up on God and lose his faith, he never wavered. Daniel was thrown in with the lions and could have been eaten, but all he did was pray and thank God for everything, and God kept him alive by keeping those hungry lions mouths shut.

Being bitter for the things that were done to us hurts not our adversaries but ourselves. It keeps us in the prison of our own making when we decide to hold on to that hurt and seek vengeance rather than letting it go and letting our scars heal. I took the pain that was inflicted on me and used it to let my beauty shine bright.

"When we as women become fully aware of who we really are, we bare a light that FORCES DARKNESS TO FLEE."

Break Every Chain *pg. 19*[12]

---

[12] (Bradley, 2018)

13
LET YOUR BEAUTY SHINE

After every breakup, a lot of people lose themselves, feel broken, and stay broken instead of seeing the beauty in their brokenness and try to use that brokenness to help others heal as well. We should all use what we've learned from being broken. We should heal first and then use the gift of another life given to us by being a blessing to someone else who may not know how to get through their hurt and pain. Psychology has proven that only ten percent of people that have been through any kind of abuse know how to regroup and make life better, whereas the other ninety percent do not seem to know how to get through life.

In my search for finding myself and mending my brokenness, I created the "Love Yourself Foundation" page on Facebook where I post a bit of my story so it will give someone else hope. I also post daily mantras to follow, to strengthen one's self. Don't let what others do to you dim your light. Let the beauty of your brokenness shine so bright that it attracts others. Always try to be an encouragement to others who may not have the strength to move on or look forward to sunnier skies. We have a duty to ourselves and to others to share our story and show others how to speak life over their own life through positive affirmations and meditation.

In a follow-up to the love yourself page, I also created the "Overcomers and Goal Achievers" page and group. With this page I post people of the Bible or other famous people who others tried to keep down who overcame adversities to become their best selves. The group is for anyone to share their story of what they have overcame in their life that they never thought they would, how that has helped them become a better version of themselves, and what they did to get to that point.

Guard your heart from being hurt again and set boundaries so as not to get hurt again, but never be afraid to love again. Loving others start with you. By loving the most important person, YOU, first, then, and only then, will you be able to love others. There are so many women out there who let a man treat them like they are nothing and accept it, and I am here to let you know that don't just accept any old treatment. Demand how you should be treated. If you show yourself love, others will also show you the same level of love.

When you let go of the anger, the hatred, and the pain and start loving yourself unconditionally, others will as well. The only thing that can snuff out the darkest is not more darkness but **light.**

14
DAILY DEVOTIONAL AND SCRIPTURES
TO LIVE BY

These are just some of the scriptures and daily devotionals that helped me get through the tough times. These devotionals helped me to realize that God is still working undercover, and he still loves us no matter what.

Boundaries 101 by HarperCollins, Zondervan, Thomas Nelson

Help Me! I need to change my life! by Pastor Brian Houston of Hillsong Church

Hope in the Midst of Pain by James Goll and Broadstreet Publishing

How to Forgive Someone by Andrew Farley

Pray Effectively by Answers with Bayless Conley

Seeking Wisdom by Krish Dhanam and Mala Ministries

Making Wise Choices by Switch a Ministry Life Church

Dealing with Emotional Pain by Answers with Bayless Conley

Overcoming Spiritual Attack by Ryan LeStrange and Charisma House

Thankfulness by American Bible Society

God's Promises by American Bible Society

Trust by MemLok, the Bible Memory System

Acts of Repentance by Life Church

Starting Over: Your Life Beyond Regrets by WaterBrook and Multnomah and Penguin Random House

Don't Look Back by Lisa Singh

Healing the Wounded Heart by Bonnie Beardsley author of More Than Just Coffee

Proper Healing From Pain by Brittany Rust

Passion and Purpose by In Touch Ministries

Hope in the Darkness by Pastor Craig Groeschel and Life Church

Growing Through Suffering by Joni and Friends, International and Tyndale House Publishers creators of the Beyond Suffering Bible

The Battles Women Face by Whispers and Fingers

Goliath Must Fall: Winning The Battle Against Your Giants by Louie Gigilio and Harper Collins

Seven Keys to Emotional Wholeness by In Touch Ministries

I forgive you but... by Karen Jensen-Salisbury

These were just some of the devotionals that helped me get through my heartbreak and my loneliness. Some are geared more towards healing, and others helped me forgive and learn to trust again.

I have read these devotionals and scriptures repeatedly.

Louie Giglio and Harper Collins, Goliath must fall: Winning the battle against your giants helped me to understand that everyone has giants, it is just how we handle those giants is what counts. Some people put on a false persona to prove to others they are making it when they are not. Others use addiction to cope. When we feel powerless in a broken world we tend to wear false armor and hide in addictions. In reading this devotional I realized on my journey of trying to heal my hurt I was hurting myself even more. I quickly jumped into a new relationship because I wanted to prove to that person I could find someone better than him. That new relationship, that person turned out to be worse and I had to end that quickly and learn to spend more time alone. Saul told David he could not kill Goliath and instead of hiding in Saul's armor, he put away all of Saul's negativity and chose to trust God to get him through that fight. In reading this devotional I realized I had to take off the false armor and just let my scars show because I know in the end God will see me through and I am going to make it.

Karen Jensen-Salisbury's I forgive you but...has helped me to realize that if I keep holding on to unforgiveness I will never get the blessings that belongs to me. God does not live in unforgiveness so why we are. As she stated in her devotional "harboring unforgiveness is like drinking poison and expecting the other person to die; it's not hurting the person you are holding a grudge against, it's hurting you." Being so angry and so bitter it was killing me inside. I learned I had to let go and forgive the other person to have a better life and better relationship with God.

Brittany Rust's Proper healing from pain help me to understand how to deal with my pain. It showed me that every time I think of the source of my pain to worship God like David did in the bible when he lost his son after killing Bathsheba's husband. Worship is a very important key in healing, as it takes the focus off your problem on onto our heavenly father. As it is said in Romans 12: 12, "Rejoicing in hope; patience in tribulations; continuing in prayer; these are three consistencies that will guide anyone in any storm to get us through to the other side. Brittany shared that it is not an easy task when you're going through it, but it is necessary in one's healing process. God is good no matter what so worshipping him should not stop just because I'm going through a storm.

Lisa Singh's, don't look back, is one of my favorite devotionals on this journey of healing and forgiveness. I spent so much time and energy after the wrongdoing, thinking to myself, "If only I had listened", or "what could have been", or "I should have done this." In reading this devotional however, it taught me to never look back and think on those things because God does not make mistakes. It showed me that I should be grateful for now and the bright future God has to me, because trust and believe he does have something greater in store for me. Lisa made it clear that our memory is not the enemy, it is the way we use our memory that will determine our detriment. Why look back when God has allowed that thing to pass to save me from a future filled with nothing but more hurt and pain. She showed me in her devotional that when I look back, look back for the mere reason of seeing where God brought me from and seeing what God did and how he has brought me through. The one thing that caught my eye with what she said was, "looking back and living in the past constantly is a clear indication you believe your treasures are still buried there." I do not want to be like Lot's wife and look back on a man and keep thinking I could have still change. I am thankful to God that he has a great future in store for me and I push forward towards that future.

I did this next devotional because one, I thought something was wrong with me and two, because I thought there were some things, I needed to change about myself to be better for me and the person God blesses me with. Pastor Brian Houston of Hillsong's, help me! I need to change, was one of the devotionals I chose to help me learn what I need to do to change my ways, change my thinking, change my life. The reward of change is the blessings of Jesus Christ. We must be willing to change certain things in our lives for a better outcome. Change is not easy, but it is possible with hard work and determination. We must be willing to accept change when the opportunity presents itself, rather than making excuses as to why we can't. As Pastor Brian stated, "Change begins with the decision to change." This is so very true. There are so many people that keep on doing wrong to others repeatedly and blaming that person for their downfall, when all they need to do is look in the mirror and ask themselves, "what do I need to change about me." I had to swallow that hard pill re-examine myself and ask, "what do I need to change about me."

"Beloved, if God so loved us, we ought also to love one another. No man hath seen God at any time. If we love one another, God dwelleth in us, and his love is perfected in us."

-     1 John 4:11-12 (KJV)

"Love is patient, love is kind. It does not envy, it does not boast, it is not proud. It does not dishonor others, it is not self-seeking, it is not easily angered, it keeps no record of wrongs. Love does not delight in evil but rejoices with the truth. It always protects, always trusts, always hopes, always perseveres. Love never fails. But where there are prophecies, they will cease; where there are tongues, they will be stilled; where there is knowledge, it will pass away."

- 1 Corinthians 13:4-8 (NIV)

"And now these three remain: faith, hope and love. But the greatest of these is love."

- 1 Corinthians 13:13 (KJV)

"Every good gift and every perfect gift are from above, and cometh down from the Father of lights, with whom is no variableness, neither shadow of turning."

- James 1:17 (KJV)

"He health the broken in heart, and bindeth up their wounds."

- Psalms 147:3 (KJV)

"Blessed be God, even the Father of our Lord Jesus Christ, the Father of mercies, and the God of all comfort; who comforteth us in all our tribulation, that we may be able to comfort them which are in any trouble, by the comfort wherewith we ourselves are comforted of God. For as the sufferings of Christ abound in us, so our consolation also aboundeth by Christ."

- 2 Corinthians 1:3-5 (KJV)

"Whoever dwells in the shelter of the Most High will rest in the shadow of the Almighty. I will say of the Lord, "He is my refuge and my fortress, my God, in whom I trust"."

- Psalms 91:1-2 (NIV)

"The Lord is my strength and my defense; he has become my salvation."

- Psalms 118:14 (NIV)

"Let all bitterness, and wrath, and anger, and clamour, and evil speaking, be put away from you, with all malice: and be ye kind one to another, tenderhearted, forgiving one another, even as God for Christ's sake hath forgiven you."

- Ephesians 4:31-32 (KJV)

"Make a joyful noise unto the Lord, all ye lands. Serve the Lord with gladness: come before his presence with singing. Know ye that the Lord he is God: it is he that hath made us, and not we ourselves; we are his people, and the sheep of his pasture. Enter into his gates with thanksgiving, and into his courts with praise be thankful unto him and bless his name. For the Lord is good; his mercy is everlasting; and his truth endureth to all generations."

- Psalms 100:1-5 (KJV)

"Forget the former things; do not dwell on the past. See, I am doing a new thing! Now it springs up; do you perceive it? I am making a way in the wilderness and streams in the wasteland."

- Isaiah 43:18-19 (NIV)

"Be careful for nothing; but in everything by prayer and supplication with thanksgiving let your requests be made known unto God. And the peace of God, which passeth all understanding, shall keep your hearts and minds through Christ Jesus."

- Philippians 4:6-7 (KJV)

"The Lord God is my strength, and he will make my feet like hind's feet, and he will make me to walk upon mine high places."

- Habakkuk 3:19 (KJV)

"Rejoicing in hope; patients in tribulation; continuing instant in prayer;"

- Romans 12:12 (KJV)

"And you, being dead in your sins and the uncircumcision of your flesh, hath the quickened together with him, having forgiven you all trespasses;"

- Colossians 2:13 (KJV)

"Wherefore if any man is in Christ, he is a new creature: the old things are passed away; behold, they are become new."

- 2 Corinthians 5:17 (ASV)

"I call heaven and earth to witness against you this day, that I have set before thee life and death, the blessing and the curse: therefore choose life, that thou mayest live, thou and thy seed;"

- Deuteronomy 30:19 (ASV)

15
DAILY AFFIRMATION

These affirmations of self-love, self-discovery, and self-encouragement were written by me. They were originally written to encourage myself that everything happened for a reason and everything would eventually be okay. God does not give us more than we can handle. He gives us just enough to test our strength to see if we have what it takes to make it. I hope these encourage someone else.

Tell yourself that;

I now willingly release all negative beliefs about myself, my life and all other people. I now forgive myself for all my wrongdoings. I am now filled with the love and the power that I am a queen, beautiful and intelligent and I will treat myself as such. All good things are now flowing into my life.

I am uniquely made, and I am like no other. I Love who I am, and I will never try to by like anyone or envy anyone else. If God wanted me to be the same, he would have created me like everyone else. I will stop beating up the most important person: **Myself.**

I will never think that anyone is better than me or that I am better than anyone. Being different from one another is what makes me who I am. I will love the person that I am. I have changed my state of mind and know that I am the woman God made me to be. Positive thinking brings about positive change.

I am royalty. I will not let anyone dim my light. The love I deserve starts with me. It is within me. I will open my mind and heart to receive the love I have for myself so I can find the love God has for me. I will **be the love I want.**

It is not what other's think of me, but what I think of myself that matters. I am my meanest yet strongest critic because no matter what anyone else says, their opinion doesn't overpower my truth.

These other affirmations can go for both men and women;

"Hey, beautiful lady (winking and blowing kisses). You are awesome, and I love you to the moon and back. Have a blessed day."

"Hey there, Mr. Handsome (flexing muscles). You have arrived; you are awesome. You are handsome; you are it. Now go out there and show the world who we are."

By starting your day with love and encouragement, you are bound to love yourself more and more. Therefore, you will eventually mean it.

Beautiful people; always walk with your head high. Never let anyone catch you with your head bowed unless it is to pray. Why? Because when you walk with your head low, it gives them the notion that you are easy to walk over and easy to take advantage of. We need to set boundaries for ourselves and never give all our power to anyone: man, woman, child, friend, or family. Sometimes when we give the other person in a relationship all our power, they tend to take advantage of it and disrespect you without taking into consideration your feelings. Setting boundaries let these abusers know what they do cannot affect the way you feel, nor will they take away your happiness. Whether it is a romantic relationship, friendship, family, or whatever, **never give one person all your power**. Leave room for disappointment so that when you are disappointed, it does not hit you hard; you can at least see it coming. When you set boundaries, no one can take advantage of you because they will understand what you will take and what you will not stand for. Kings and queens do not bow; they want to avoid their crown falling off so stand tall, adjust your crown, and be bowed to.

A person's mistakes don't necessarily mean that they are good or bad; it just means we're all humans capable of making mistakes. However, the way you treat yourself tells a person just how you see yourself. Give yourself some credit and know you are deserving of your own love and so much more.

The heart can either be the strongest muscle in your body or the weakest. Your heart can either lie to you or tell you the truth. **Jeremiah 17:9 states, "The heart is deceitful above all things and beyond cure. Who can understand it?"** Your heart can be your enemy, and it can be your friend. **Proverbs 4:23 reads, "Above all else, guard your heart, for everything you do flows from it."** It's your choice.

Negative self-talk will also make you think that everyone else who means you no harm is also talking about you. The mind can be either your enemy or your friend. You are the one that wields the pen; you control your own mind. Think positive thoughts and watch your life change for the better. Let the devil play tricks with your mind, and you will reap the benefits of the negative thoughts you are thinking.

Fear and hope go hand in hand like a cloak and dagger. When fear lies to you and show you its darkest lies, hope tells you the truth and shows you the opposite. The one thing that's an intermediate to fear and hope is faith. Without having just, a bit of faith, fear will always choke out hope. Don't let fear stop you from hoping, and always have faith that you will accomplish what you hope for.

Loving yourself doesn't just mean showing your physical self some love but also your mental self. Too many people walk around with mental scars, beating themselves up internally instead of giving themselves a chance. First rule in loving yourself is learning to forgive yourself for the wrong things you've done or that was done to you. When you have truly forgiven yourself, you will be able to see yourself in the best light and see the love you deserve.

One's throne is not made of diamonds or riches. One's status as a royal is not dependent on what family one is born into or who one marries. We are all royals in our own right because our heavenly father has made us such. We need to lift our heads high and know we are royalty. We need to walk and talk like we know that we are royalty. Never let anyone make you feel like you are less that what your heavenly father says you are. Man does not define who we are or who we will become; God does. Every day you open your eyes, the first person you see is yourself. If you see yourself as a nobody, that is what will be reflected. Give yourself a chance at life and prove yourself wrong by first loving who you are and who you can be.

"I love you girl." That is what I tell myself daily. God gave me eyes to see the beauty in everything he created, and the first beauty I see when I wake up and walk to my mirror is ME. I love you girl.

I fell in love today all over again. I fell in love with the mind, the body, and the soul. I fell in love with the character, the loving heart, and the sense of humor. I fell in love with the talk, the walk, the poise, and the intelligence. She blushes as I admire just how much I love her passion, fire, drive for success, self-discovery, and self-worth. I've never met anyone so genuine and so beautiful until I discover her. Her name? Her name is royalty. Her name is worthy. Her name is the proverbs 31 woman. Her name is Valencia Michelle Dore.

ACKNOWLEDGMENTS

This book would not have been possible without God. If I didn't put my trust in him or have a little faith, I don't think I would have made it this far. A very heartfelt thank you to both my mother and father, Laurena Millard and Michael Dore, for always believing in me and encouraging me to harness my talents and be the best version of myself. Thanks to my stepmother and very inspirational woman of God, Joy Dore, for always praying for me, believing in me, looking out for me, and basically being my guardian angel. You always have a word of wisdom for me from our creator.

To members of my family who think that I may think that I am better than them, so I have to show them up, I am sorry; I didn't mean to make anyone feel like I'm better than them because I am only better than myself from yesterday. Although we haven't always gotten along and the support was not there for me as I would have wanted it to be, I'm still very much thankful for it because it made me grind harder. It made me want to be better than people said or thought I could be. It gave me the motivation to work harder to make my dream a reality.

To my pastors, Agnola Martin and Daniel, for trying their best to help me and believing in my marriage, even when they too could have seen it was doomed from the start because *he* did not believe in me and did not believe in us. My pastors prayed for me and kept me afloat when I felt like death was knocking at my door because of the difficulty I was going through.

Thanks to my brother and his wife for their support and understanding through this transition. Thank you for giving my children and me a place to lay our heads when we had no place to go. We are eternally grateful. I'm so happy to share this book with you.

To my wonderful sister, Tia Walker, and my adopted mother, Elaine Mise, for all the love and encouragement. Mom, I know you tried to warn me a long time ago but just like a bullheaded teenager, I just wanted to learn the hard way, I guess. Sorry I didn't tell you earlier on what was going on, but I wanted to tell you in person. Glad I was able to talk it out with you and still had your love and support afterward.

To my girl, Erin Bottley, my Asian compadre, Eric Dy, my girl Veronica and my Booski, James Crouch, the original AutoZone #3017 squad, for being that voice of constant encouragement. They knew what I was going through and always had an uplifting word of encouragement for me. I will forever love you guys. You guys are like family to me.

To my girl, Alicia Solomon, even though you never really came out and said, "he's no good for you", I always understood your questions about my decisions with him. Through it all you have still been there even after everything he put me through, and I am very grateful.

To my girl, Tish Jacobs, for having my back. She literally told him when we were getting married that if he screwed up, she would reach for him, and I knew she would too. She can relate to my problem because we both marry men from the same area, and they both turned out to be jack-of-all-trades.

To my best friend, Lemuel Ryan. I know, at times, it seemed like I threw you away, but you understood it was not you; it was the situation I was in. You were always there for me since I met you in 2008 and always have been. Thank you for opening your doors to my children and I when tragedy struck us in December of 2018. If it weren't for you being there through the whole ordeal and giving us a place to stay, I do not know where we would have been. I am forever grateful for your love and support.

To my crazy Hispanic amigo, mi Corazon, Hansel Croft, for being that one crazy friend who is willing to take a jail for me. He was always cursing me out and telling me to get out of the relationship or he will drag me out. Through all the craziness and through all the jokes and the tears, he was serious about beating someone to a pulp for messing with me. Thank you, my love, for hanging tight with me since 2006. The day I met you, I knew you were a forever friend and a true one.

To the woman and her child who took my kindness for weakness and tried their best to break me down to nothing, I thank you. It is because of your betrayal why I am stronger now than I was then. If it wasn't for your betrayal, I would not have found the strength to walk away from a marriage that was dead before it even started.

Thanks to the man that didn't know my value or my worth for attempting to destroy my kind heart. If it wasn't for you being a chronic cheater, a liar, manipulator, and not knowing the good thing you had in front of you, I don't think I would have had the strength to finally tell you to go to hell. I gave you seven good years, and you took it all for granted. I was your right hand, and you left me without one. I was your body, and you left me dead from the neck down. You took every ounce of kindness and every love I had for you, and you shredded it to pieces. But I am here to thank you for doing so because you have made room for the real man God has for me.

<u>ENDNOTE</u>

Ally, D. (2019). *About: Daniel Ally*. Retrieved from Daniel Ally: https://www.danielally.com/about

Bradley, K. (2018). *Break Every Chain.* Independently Published.

Dahl Silver, K. (2019). My Prayer Journal: Bible Encouragement for Hope and Healing. In K. D. Silver, *My Prayer Journal* (pp. 60-61). Ohio: Barbour Publishing.

Jackson, A. (2006). *Lyrics: Turn Your Eyes Upon*. Retrieved from AZ Lyrics: https://www.azlyrics.com/lyrics/alanjackson/turnyoureyesuponjesus.html

JoyBell, C. (2015). *Quotes: Goodreads*. Retrieved from Goodreads: https://www.goodreads.com/quotes/7006732-in-this-life-we-reap-the-results-of-everything-that

Mandela, N. (2011). *Field Notes: Everyday Ambassador*. Retrieved from Everyday Ambassador: http://everydayambassador.org/2015/07/20/nelson-mandelas-three-life-rules/

Niebuhr, R. (n.d.). *Internet Resources*. Retrieved from Sky Designs:

http://skdesigns.com/internet/articles/prose/niebuhr/serenity

_prayer/

Nietzsche, F. (n.d.). *Everyday Power*. Retrieved from Everyday Power:

https://everydaypower.com/friedrich-nietzsche-quotes/

Park, R. (n.d.). *Rosa Park Facts*. Retrieved from

http://rosaparksfacts.com/rosa-parks-quotes/

Robinson, D. (n.d.). *Quotes: Meditative Mind*. Retrieved from Meditative

Mind: https://meditativemind.org/daily-mindfulness-quotes-

017-meditation-prayer/

Smedes, L. B. (1997). The Art of Forgiving. In L. B. Smedes, *The Art of

Forgiving* (p. 71). New York: Ballantine Books.

Unknown. (2016). *Live Life Happy*. Retrieved from Live Life Happy:

https://livelifehappy.com/life-quotes/take-life-day-day-

grateful/

ABOUT THE AUTHOR

Valencia Michelle Dore was born on a small island in the Caribbean called the federation of St. Kitts and Nevis. In 1998 her family migrated to the United Stated Virgin Islands. In 2000 she joined the United States Air Force. After the military Valencia decided to work towards her goal of earning her bachelor's degree in Information Technology. In 2010 she was able to accomplish that goal. Valencia went on to continue with her education even with being the mother of a toddler and a 9-year-old. She received her Master's in Information Technology in 2011 and a second Bachelor's in Paralegal Studies in 2015. Being the mother of three beautiful gifts, she hardly has the time between work and them, but she made the time for school. Currently she is attending Northcentral University for her Doctorate in Business Administration in Information Technology. Before she overcame heartbreak, betrayal, abuse and failure, she was a very depressed individual with suicidal tendencies. It is her hope through her book and other books to come, to be an inspiration to other abused women. She would like to help them learn how to heal their broken self, to know that they are beautiful to having been broken. Since she was a little girl, she always knew that God had a purpose and a plan for her life. Now it is up to her to positioning herself to walk into that plan and purpose. It is her hope to launch her own non-profit organization that will help young girls and women love themselves more. Therefore, she created the Love Yourself Foundation.

Made in the USA
Monee, IL
18 March 2020